PASSION & PAIN

Poems, Prayers and Thoughts from the Soul

D. L. Mahan

About the Author

D. L. Mahan is the author of several books ranging from historical, spiritual, poetry and mystery novels; and he is a graduate of ministry from Wagner University. He is married with one son and a grandfather of six. He spends most of his time in Palm Springs, California and Colorado.

To Brandy and Deb

Table of Contents

Children of Shame 1

Family Legacy 2

Poet Inspired 4

Passerby in Barren Woods 6

Noble Trade 8

For a World Full of Hope 9

Where Did I Go to Die 10

Twilight Hour 11

Undone 12

Royal Oak Haunting 13

The Returning 14

Winter's Nap 16

Oak Tree 17

Joshua 18

Heaven's Door 20

Impressions 21

Unfettered 21

Unhinged 22

The Offering 22

Love Not Taken 23

Freedom (Hope) 24

The Hill 26

Man of Sorrows 27

The War Within 28

Summer's Friend 29

Gratitude 30

Thankful Prayer 31

Seasons 32

Gathering at Harvest 34

Soul Mate 35

Santa Fe.. 36

Regret.. 38

Sanctuary Misplaced... 39

Gone Cherry Picking... 40

The Counterfeit... 42

Gravesite Discourse.. 43

Autumn's Dance.. 44

The Woodchopper.. 46

Wedding Day... 47

Grandchildren.. 48

The Giant... 49

Insatiable... 50

An Island Visited by Many Ships.. 51

The Good Fight.. 52

My Disappointment, When She Visits Me... 53

Biography of Lucifer... 54

Misdirected Rage.. 56

Essay on Grief... 57

Hope Renewed... 59

A Beautiful Riot.. 60

Paradise Found.. 62

Essay on Purpose.. 63

Eulogy of A Tree... 64

Words Unspoken.. 66

Postulation... 68

Alone, My Song Sings Loudly.. 69

Free Will.. 70

Colorado Christmas... 71

Essay on Affirmation and Attitude.. 72

A Tribute to Dave.. 73

Thoreau's Vision... 75

Children of Shame

Something there is that owns a child, that trades their pride for false guilt

And perhaps for life remain beguiled, with fear misplaced and often built.

Their hearts lay burdened with no just plea; transgressions are another thing

For that is guilt owned honestly, redemption paid for everything.

Yet, tormented souls, morose and driven, their strength is spent on vain remorse

And futile search for selves forgiven, martyrs by name, though children, of course.

They sing their anthem loud and clear: "I shall accept the blame for naught."

Though naught begot naught, and shame begets fear

And children make poor scapegoats.

Their forebears denied and refused to accept,

Their guilt and consequence.

Unwilling to own their err or sin,

Thus, offspring now to recompense.

For she is love unfaithful, and I am man once killed!

Each hidden stain and blemish truthful, a hallowed secret never willed.

Hence image saved and cherished dear, though casualties surrender self

Fettered by chains of shame and fear, for acceptance now deny thyself.

Yes, children make poor scapegoats.

Though battlefield be ever known,

Their souls are cloaked with threats now sown.

Unaware of ghost in closet hid, till time when all shall be revealed

Then learn they must all shame to rid, with guilt returned — esteem thus sealed,

For children make poor scapegoats.

Family Legacy

We go walking arm in arm, that frost chilled morn, between the snow-laden pines, and

I ask, "Are you mine?"

You give my hand a shake to promise there is no mistake.

And I return a squeeze in kind, betwixt the cedar and the pine.

At the village up ahead, we stop for a loaf of sour bread.

The baker's shop smells sweet of ginger, and you inquire, "Can we linger?"

The family's at the cabin, awaiting our return – generations yet to teach,

But we have much still to discern. And understanding, now to reach.

To understand where our paths diverged, and why our hearts grew cold, apart.

"Why," I ask, "to our word, did we depart?"

We smile both sheepishly, then take the other in long embrace.

As words of love fill the air, time stands still, thus...no need to race.

It is in those moments cherished dear, we know the other's affection, clear –

And the sacred bond that held us orphans near.

We bring to mind the creed of old: family, faith and courage bold.

We talk of storms we weathered and of the plans we laid –

And the far too simple action of the promises we made.

It is then the culprit 'comes so clear: the tame outsider lurking near –

Life's hectic schedule, for which to steer.

Ah, when to the heart of family was it ever less than betrayal,

To forget to cherish time, and life so very frail

Or look the other way and ignore the outsider's assail?

Then on that snow packed trail we venture home; for home is where loved ones be known.

For as the moonlit woods are truly deep, we have covenant now, anew to keep.

We pledge ourselves once again: to be family, blood and ever friend.

The twilight hour will soon descend –

And we have legacy and love to mend,

Yes, we have legacy and love to mend.

Poet Inspired

I went to place

Of hollow green

In hopes it would

Provoke me thought,

For trees of pine

Surround in care

And rolling hills

Of grass do say,

"Come sit and breathe

In life aware."

So, sit I did

Betwixt the trees

And bid the words

Of life to fall

Upon my soul

For all to hear

The gifts of God:

Immortal thought,

Beheld with love

And cherished dear.

Now go I still

To place of verse

And homage pay

To nature's worth;

Then take, in turn,

An image felt

Of fallen leaf

Or flower's birth.

Hence, deep within

This poet dwelt.

Passerby in Barren Woods

When on my steed

One winter's eve,

I came across

A dying leaf

Who urged me so

To stay and mend

His withered frame

Soon to descend

I vexed him for

The reason why

So reluctant

He was to die

He stared at me

As though I jest,

And said he had

No need for rest

I thought it strange

That he remain,

When all his kin

Had long since lain

Insist he did

His life not o'er,

Though useful be

He seemed no more

Then thought it best

His time now end,

With stroke of hand

His death to lend

While riding on

I felt such grief

For one reluctant

Now dead leaf.

Noble Trade

The old man stands hardened as flint – he waits for the younger one

The one who knows everything, yet knows nothing at all

They chat for a moment – then pride drives the wedge

The hammer; the chisel; the saw; and the wrench –

These are his hands – old, weathered and worn

The elder still wanting to teach – the subject: the wood, the steel and concrete

The lad is taken by his master's esteem – of the scars he bears

Scars the lad cannot pretend to bear, nor eagerness quench

He must wait now. He must become hardened as flint

As humility is the greatest instructor, reality is the greatest classroom

For the lad must learn from the pain – his own mistakes

Time is his friend. Yet his master's foe: Death's foul stench.

For a World Full of Hope

For a world full of hope, yet seldom seen, I breathe in the blessing of grace exchanged...

I observe the elderly man stop to offer encouragement to the young boy striving for equanimity after the bully walks away.

I watch as the African American woman is defended by the southern white officer as the bigot's harassment is halted.

I drink in the heartening sight as the conservative and liberal politicians shake hands in agreement on a common, noble cause.

Yet, knowing these hopeful moments are but fleeting foreshadows of what we *could* become,
I pray the God of us all would instill in humanity the yearning for love, and true altruism.

Where Did I Go to Die

Where did I go that day to die? In meadow green or ocean deep

And at the end of suffering's cry, did I my soul then pray to keep?

Or did I leave this earthly place, with heartbeat fast, for fear to rid

And head hung low in deep disgrace; for coward in some cavern hid?

Was it with friendship rich in love that I departed temporal plane?

Or was it with no thought above, empty, alone, and with disdain?

And was the place where I last fell, turned into shrine or sacred ground?

Or was it feared and shame to tell, if ever there you could be found?

I hope it was in battle fierce, that I laid down my soul to rest.

With cold steel sword through heart did pierce, to grant me die of courage – best.

Where did I go to die that day? When reaper came with sickle raised

A place of pride and honor pray, where men who went before were praised.

Twilight Hour

I went walking by that golden pond – as the day's light was dying just outside

I had for my twilight stroll beyond, my terrier and hiking stick – my memories beside

Remembering a time long since passed – of family, love, and friendship fast

I wandered off the trail laid there. And knew not how or sufficiently where,

The path would lead, or if returned, I'd ever see the dawn of day.

Yet since I knew the faithful birch, the sturdy oak – would, long since gone, outlast

I took it in (God's grand design), and ventured out with pleasure, miles more

Till all I knew would come to naught – replaced with sanctified peace restored.

My ally gave his leash a shake, to see if I had made mistake

Insisted I, we forge ahead – sojourners in this time – till dead.

As hours passed, and twilight fell, I knew our fate would soon foretell:

When walking in the dusk of day, embrace the past, but learn the way.

David. L. Mahan 11

Undone

As I breathe in Your presence – enthralled by Your glory

My heart is undone by Your love and Your mercy.

You have raptured my soul, engendered a worship

A heart song of praise – for You, to accept.

O LORD, – lover of my soul – I am undone by Your passion, engrossed in Your majesty

Tasting of Your goodness and gazing at Your beauty, my heart is surrendered – You are so holy!

You dance with me upon waters of change, stirring me on to be all that You claim:

Whole in Your presence, alive in Your Name.

You are my hiding place, my mighty fortress

My life and saving grace, my hope, eternal rest.

Let Your endless grace wash over me, saturate me with Your Spirit

May a hunger grow within my heart, a longing to endear it.

I delight myself in You, LORD – in the splendor of Your sovereignty

For You alone are from everlasting to eternity.

Forgive me for the times I have failed to behold You, blinded by pride, fear, and regret

Instill in me now Your life to renew, capture my heart – Your love to reflect.

Royal Oak Haunting

We left our home, the home filled with hope and love – and yes, bitter pain

We set out from there needing to forge ahead. A dream cloaked in fear.

Our path was unknown, both to young and old, though cleverly feigned

We told our lies, held our secrets close. Our fresh start, unclear.

You made your voice known, and sounded the cry, "We should've stayed back there!"

Though our elders' response: "Too late to return. The ships, already burnt."

"We have to make the best of this new world," they said. "Know that we care."

But caring wasn't enough. The illness and shame we had packed – still current.

Dependency was our master. And we were its slave.

"I needed you to define me." You needed me the same.

For fear of the dying, the loss, and the grave

We silenced the truth and accepted the blame.

So the haunting commenced – each playing our part

Like ghosts that were tormented, we lived out the lie.

Though united we were, both soul and the heart,

Till elders were gone – and grief was undone – hence, regret now bely.

David. L. Mahan 13

The Returning

My hiding heart stirred at the thought of return

Return to the home,

Not of birth nor of learned

The place where ancestors of old now lay

Lay at rest in the earth, "Peace," solemnly pray

A home not of knowledge,

Nay, home not of mind

In spirit now searching,

Of blood, same of kind

Though Heaven be true home,

And this day now unfurling

I fix my stride, hence,

To their past memories clinging

Why soul are you yearning?

Pining dreams of ole yore

Awaken thine reason,

Forbid me before

O' ransomed life dare, take

Hold of what have thee

And save not regret,

Nor bargain thy victory

David. L. Mahan 14

For now is the time, then

Too late e'er to sing

Entreat my wretched soul,

For Serenity returning.

Winter's Nap

I had for my weekend stay, a chance to sleep the 'noon away.

The outdoor chores of chopping wood and pruning maple,

Will wait till after 'morrow's storm doth enable

The way to leave those toilsome cares behind,

And in return, entreat some rapturous dreams in kind

Of winter's day, with frosted panes and snow-capped hills,

Yet warm and safe inside, save only selfish thrill

Was fate's sweet chance to rest and take a vict'ry lap....

Upon my chair for a long winter's nap.

David. L. Mahan 16

Oak Tree

Come to the oak tree all ye who play

While time is still no matter,

For what today seems trivial

Tomorrow will wear and tatter.

And if your heart be heavy laden

Enslaved to daily grind,

Then climb upon its loyal branches

And youthful ways do find.

For wish I did, to ne'er grow old

Thus, grow old never did

'Twould be a shame when come to end

Youth found in closet hid.

So come to my tree – or come to yours,

But most important, come

And climb and sing, and live aloud

The silent shadow's sum.

David. L. Mahan 17

Joshua

Through the eyes of wonder

See the need to know,

Grasping every moment

Wanting so to grow

Character emerging

Developing a will,

Exploring all his boundaries

Needing limits still

Lacking understanding

Striving though to gain

A glimpse of the reason

Why freedom unattained

No pleasure for granted taken

Each joy in life, still new,

A lesson for the older

To taste life's sweetness too

Each failure is for learning

Then getting on with life,

Instead of them reliving

Causing only strife

David. L. Mahan 18

His simple ways of showing

The honesty of his pain,

For us the obligation

Our feelings to refrain

Mistake me not

Lest you perceive

That I am saying

His ways all receive

Not that our lives

Anew we start,

But that we live

Young at heart.

David. L. Mahan 19

Heaven's Door

That roadside marker, their gravesites be

The door to Heaven ever beckoning me

I came upon that tiny village today,

In search of truth, dispelling fearful ways

Hoping to find evidence, cogent

To put to rest my postulation, bent

For while some are waiting their resting place,

Others are wishing they espoused lasting grace

Hence, loved ones departed this ephemeral plane

Renouncing my loss – Rejoicing, their gain

For witness did see their spirits to rise

Ascending to home, eternal in skies

Reminiscent of Elijah in chariot of old,

Did my ancestors leave with faith deeply bold

Now I am content, their peace e'er a must

Yet I am alone, with my wanderlust.

David. L. Mahan 20

Impressions

Notions of nonsense invade my mind, like birds flying overhead.

Yet I am grounded – I am sane; I am far from dead.

So, I shall take these fallacies and make them captive, hence;

These battlefields, like robins' nests, shall never be entrenched.

Unfettered

Do you recall that Autumn's night

When howled the wind undaunted?

And I, the child, embraced my fright,

'Twas then that fear revealed to sight

For we, the children, haunted.

Hence, days have passed and years reflect,

Since in my youth did tremble

Yet have I still for fear respect,

And hope that ne'er I shall detect

A lack of there resemble.

For reverence lost, is wisdom slain

Upon the altar - folly

But Godly fear once seen, to then attain,

A sense of awe, a sense of pain

Shall grant thy soul be free.

David. L. Mahan 21

Unhinged

At dawn's first light, my wife gave a scream

An ear-piercing pitch with a startling fright,

She'd never once before to rouse.

I rushed to the pantry, her life to esteem

Beholding the reason – most ghastly of sight:

That scared little scampering mouse.

The Offering

At moments like these, when hearts are laid bare

As a shipwreck hull, battered and rent

For all to behold – yet none offer care

I swallow my pride, lay hold of time spent

And beckon you in, knowing how and the where

(I vanquish my guard, demolish my walls)

And you enter in, my soul to now mend.

Love Not Taken

She came in beauty, of soul and heart
She spoke of faithful, ne'er torn apart

'Twas I, reluctant, her love receive
'Twas I, the fool, who bid her leave

Her offering but, a selfless act
Her motive pure, no grace did lack

As though unworthy, the gift too great
As though self loathe, did seal my fate

And with her love, birthed honesty
And from her heart, reality

Yet I was doubtful, such love exist
Yet I was hopeful, she would persist

Now I, forlorn, her gift deny
Now she the richer, to pass me by.

David. L. Mahan 23

Freedom (Hope)

If I could stop
The hands of time
To envelop life
With wit and rhyme

For it seems we are
Pulled by the hand
Through life's hourglass
Ne'er full of sand

Yes, I doubt that I
Shall ever see
A day that truly stands
Still, just for me

A day for work
A day for play,
Free from worry
Ne'er slips away

To work the land
And hold the plow,
To smell the earth
And long for it now

David. L. Mahan 24

To be at home

In open fields

To find my strength

From all it yields

For no other place

Pray there be,

Where time is servant

And I am free.

David. L. Mahan 25

The Hill

I climbed that hill today, away from home, not far away

For curious was I to see, if grass was greener on other side be

Leaving behind friends, clan and kin, telling myself ne'er wanted back in

I stood atop and looked below, down at the village now filled with snow

Then turned around, and looking back, I saw no window but that was black.

I trekked toward hamlet below, yet wrestled with my memories so

As I approached the first full row of houses nestled all in snow,

I took a glimpse through curtains hanging, of gatherings with townsfolk singing

But gazing back, none seeing me

Gave wave, or smile, or recognized be.

I knew at once the cost I paid: the love at home I gave away

I vowed and repented, but starting back, I feared they would not bid me stay

Now journey ending, at front door stood I

I knocked and pleaded, then gave a cry.

Soon, neighbor I had once next door

Came up to me, to him implore,

"Where hath my family gone, do tell."

His sullen stare I knew too well

He told of how, moved on, had they

He said he knew not of which way

With pity felt, he offered help

With full remorse, my barbaric yelp.

Man of Sorrows

Born in humility, yet King e'er to be

Man, in His likeness, yet

Godhead of three

He came with a mission; He came in God's plan:

Redemption, forgiveness, salvation at hand

Enjoined us His call, for all to believe

His sorrows and grief, now He shall receive

Through Cross did He die on that old shameful hill,

O' empty tomb . . . did He win!

Removing all shame and made pardon for sin

So, offer Him homage, worship and praise

Our Savior is worthy, hence new life to raise!

David. L. Mahan 27

The War Within

I sat there in my reading loft, content to try and write . . .

Instead, deciphered more of Frost;

For words of wisdom descend upon my heart tonight,

And beckon me to count the cost:

The cost of how I bargained peace

Away, for fleeting guard –

Against the fear, and pain's release

In turn, now faith retard;

Yet faith is where my hope shall stand,

And trust is dread's real foe.

Thus, I relented, and have succumbed to reason now embrace,

The truth of who thine ally is: God's e'er unchanging grace.

Grace freely lavished and unearned,

Dispelling doubts' charade.

His love poured out upon that Tree,

'Twas ransom gladly paid.

Now studied I, the price He paid:

The sacrifice Love made;

And how that Love, hence perfectly –

Now casts my fears away.

Summer's Friend

My summer's friend was Brandy,
Kind maiden sweet as candy

Her outlook ever faithful,
Her heart was ever grateful

For she was in her heaven,
When summer's end would deafen

Days that lengthen, never ending
Love extended, ne'er unbending

She saw the beauty in the dawn,
And basked in sunset's vibrant song

The crashing waves and seagulls' ease,
The simple joys, she gladly sees

Though I was foolish, to ne'er detect
The glory of her wonder and why she wept

In ignorance, I bid her leave
For fear of love, I chose to grieve

Still, she was gracious, ne'er love to end
And she was faithful, my summer's friend.

David. L. Mahan 29

Gratitude

When the whip-poor-will sings its song at night,

Though I am not for whom it sings – still I am blessed nonetheless.

And while, in times of spiteful discourse, though rebuff be my earn'd lot

Grateful was I for Your tender caress.

That sun-drenched day, I stole a glance as the mare and her colt exchanged affection,

Lovingly, down by the riverbanks.

And I declare the God for whom I praise, though transgress just the same,

Is worthy of all my thanks!

I hear the sound of a world gone bye, an innocence lost in a troubled sea

Yet I am here, still, and so are you; that life exists, and identity.

This prodigious sonata extends, with grace, mercy, and love

For you and for me doth blessings abound, from Heaven above.

Thankful Prayer

"Father God, I thank You for every good and perfect gift that comes from Your hand.

You have blessed me abundantly in many ways, such I could ne'er recount how grand!

Thank You, Father, for Your faithfulness, loving-kindness, mercy, and grace.

I praise You for healing, protection, love, and favor – ne'er to erase.

I declare everything I am and have comes from You.

For this I know is true, it all belongs to You.

Help me to be a faithful steward with an ever-grateful heart.

I'll worship You in my giving and serving, from life's blessed start.

Help me reflect Your lavish generosity and love,

In how I bless others with my talents and treasures from above.

And with no captious motive nor intent,

Let me behold the beggar as friend, cogent

In the wonderful name of Jesus, amen."

Seasons

The last lone oak leaves came rattling down

Proclaiming their death

As they kissed the cold ground

And you were reminded of a love unreturned

Long since surrendered

Of pain and regret learned

Then baren and grey

Did the earth now reflect

Echoing loss felt

No hope there detect

So, stayed in that place

Of snow fallen new

Till emptiness traded

For promises, through

Now I am the pitied

For spring hath been born

Yet, you are the better

For I bear the scorn

New life all around me

Ne'er I to perceive

Engulfed in my pride

Hence bid me to leave

Now summer has opened

New chance for rebirth

Choices descending

Like dew on the earth

Thus, I will choose love

For as days are as long

Hence, I will seek out

My beauty and song

Lessons are learned now

Dog days are gone

Refreshing fall breeze,

Ushers in our new dawn.

Gathering at Harvest

Nothing evokes feelings of life on a farm, like harvest time – Its simple ways, honest grace, and kindred charm.

The cool, brisk autumn air disseminating life, and that natural "bovine blessing"
Dispelling all struggles of summer – torrential storms and heat e'er distressing.

Now, that refreshing fall breeze reminds us those "dog days" are complete
Winter lies ahead and, with it, the hope of peaceful retreat.

But first, it's time to bring forth the fruits of our labor. "I'll meet you at the pantry at dawn.
First share a biscuit and jam to savor."

We've done all the work to prepare for good harvest:
We've plowed the hard soil – and tilled that fallow ground, best.

We've extracted all pernicious weeds from past turpitude;
We've planted healthy fruitful seeds of praise and gratitude.

And even fertilized with the rich nutrients of friendship
Diligent to water each day with the Word, us to equip.

To protect which God had birthed in us with hallowed, fervent prayer.
And now it's time to reap what we've sown with toil and earnest care.

Wait! The crops, the fruit – they aren't what we had planned.
Our souls are still hardened – calloused, insipid, and bland.

"But what about the Sonshine of surrender?" you query.
"He alone is the radiance that makes us free from worry."

Ah, yes, our hearts should e'er be filled with effervescent joy.
But why did we miss out on that blessing to employ?

Most likely, we forgot the latter part – surrender.
That alone ensures lasting peace – engendered.

The daylight soon is dying and time is ever fleeting;
So now, must we ponder and confront – what's competing?

What surreptitious kingdoms are, we simply can't surrender?
I will sharpen you, and you can sharpen me – please be tender.

"For me, it is the land and home – I 'spect for you, your loving kin."
Either way, He wants it all – lest that foul spirit be gathering within.

Soul Mate

Setting out this dew-drenched morn, tomorrow's hike may be too late

My children do not wish me go alone, for precarious be my gait.

Yet I have someone I must meet – an old and trusted friend

I'll look for her up yonder way, around trail's upmost bend.

Perhaps she'll tarry sooner, perhaps she'll help me find

The love that joined us to each other – of spirit same in kind.

Hence, I persist, this pilgrimage, though canyon shadows fall

For hope must I now e'er insist – deny old age its steadfast gall.

Just then I came upon that fork in path, e'er dreaded vier be

That beckoned me to choose the way, to go most easily.

But she is waiting – though, she has passed

Just as these faded, trodden leaves, alas.

I think on moments shared and memories – that stir me on to last

Though uphill journey, arduous be – strength find I now, in tender past.

For I must say my heartfelt verse, now to my soulmate dear

Yes, she is worthy praise – though way less traveled be more sheer.

I sense her presence, e'er sweet and true

She stirs me on with faith anew.

At summit's end, our gaze upon God's mural quenched my heart cry, thee

This ghostly specter of pulchritude – Ever sweetly haunting me.

David. L. Mahan 35

Santa Fe

Our journey to that sacred place of legend and of lore,

Where saints and warriors bled and died, in the name of God, before.

That hallowed ground beneath the bell, where four hundred lives fought and fell,

And ancient victors lived to tell.

And though their battle o'er proselytize be,

Their ignominious fate in church's eyes did see.

So, wait several more years till Spanish conquest quelled all fears.

Still, no peace would reign nor calm be near, for nigh seven score years.

Thus, ownership would then let go, back to the old Mexico –

Old Glory's reign would have to wait, until the year forty-eight.

For first, did Kearny raise our flag in plaza made of sticks

Preparing way for Hidalgo Pact, back in forty-six.

That legendary trail, from Missouri through the Vale

Led twenty-one men of daring fame to "Siberia of Mexican Republic" name.

Those Mexican despots of old age did then arouse the farmers' rage

Rousting what we came to know, as the Rebellion Chimayo'.

And during bloody Civil War, with all the pain and bloodshed bore,

That Rebel flag flew three days, true – till taken down by men in blue.

Then in the year of '69, the priest named Lamy began in kind,

Construct that chapel with fame renown: Saint Francis Cathedral in the heart of town.

For were it not the Kid's sealed fate, the Governor Wallace would be the late.

And would no novel be then stirred, such as the famous, called Ben Hur.

Statehood gained in 1912 did bring about more fame to tell, of history, tradition and glory Grand

– of mystic hamlet within God's hand.

Hence piqued the spell of Santa Fe, prepared the passage, prepared the way –

To then with God commune the soul, through timeless beauty, praise extol.

Regret

In moments like these
> That tempt and tease

With images past
> That haunt and last

I shan't be told
> Which way to feel

By some forgotten
> Offense, though real

Or of my own willful err
> Though justified, albeit fair

You wouldn't want me waste more sense
> Them now to seek, recompense

Help me then change
> My outlook on life

Lest, I become estranged –
> Consumed with toxic strife.

Now secret learned
> New joy revealed

New hope in future earned
> In letting go – regrets once yearned

And dreaded fate once sealed

David. L. Mahan 38

Sanctuary Misplaced

I built that cabin in my mind today,

Deep in the woods – so far away

But you were not there – no love did abound,

Only bittersweet memories and emptiness found

So deeper I fled in my hiding place,

Striving my feelings of love to erase

But peace did not greet me, nor comfort did feel

Unwelcome was I and told to be real

Real to my passion, real to my pain

Embracing this plight – myself to then gain

Though haunted by love and tortured by time,

Instilled in me faith of outcome sublime

For what could be better

Than God's will be done?

'Tis only a snare when

Man's will doth run.

David. L. Mahan 39

Gone Cherry Picking

When we were both lads,

With summer in full bloom

We set out that Sunday glad,

For those cherry trees to groom.

But you were chagrined, having tried, only to fail

A chance to unite the mother you knew

With her father so frail

Said the echoes of heartache in the wind that blew.

So, we ventured instead the long way to the trees

Wanting more time to ponder, needing more time to mull

Then came a stirring of hope in that early June breeze,

And a kindling of love, more sharpened than dull.

And when we approached the first tree in line,

We went to the branches – picking only the loyal

The cherries were ready, ripened and fine

Our kingdom, the monarch! Imagined, though royal.

At moments like those, we felt so alive

We harkened the embers of dreams to arise,

Dreams that would carry to new worlds ne'er strive,

Pure rapture and joy embraced in the skies.

But those dreams had to wait,

And our joy thwarted when

We came upon man, years to the late –

Seated at tree, bereft of life then.

"My grandfather's dead!" you exclaimed with a shriek,

That day at the orchard down by the creek.

With comfort conferred, I noted in hand –

The carving of wood: an image of dove,

Recipient clear. Simple yet grand –

Your mother's name carved, engendering love.

Apparent to us, his dying wish be:

Reconciliation and peace –

Embodied in family,

With animosity ceased.

Hence years have long passed since that day of dark grief.

And you are now home where your grandfather be –

And I am the lone one, though time left be brief –

To ponder on love beside that old tree.

The Counterfeit

I'm wishing for a winter's snow, just like the ones we used to know

With morning's frost, and late day's freeze – the kind of grey wolves and late geese

The kind we spent all day inside – up in the blanket,

Content to hide

Now walk through path of flower's birth, and praise the One who gave its worth

Yet still lament for time passed by, when squandered I, earth's hibernal cry

Just yesterday, I learned to know the love for winter's fate

Between God's truth above, and mankind's soulful gate

She warned me not to yearn (my mate), for such a snowfall sum

This time of spring so very late, since yuletide's requiem

Yet, offspring now to rue the day when winter's snow be denied

Or God's true calling to delay, from fearful place of hollow lies

For no greater loss can there be, than lifetime spent on vanity

Or missed the mark on purpose made, and vain remorse for plans err laid

They shall be 'membering this with a gleam – sometime generations hence:

Joy's counterfeit to ne'er esteem – thus, no need to recompense.

Gravesite Discourse

It's time for me to leave, it's time for me to go

I wanted so to stay, and wanted so to show

My demons now are dead, and soul can rest in peace

Before the leaves have fallen, and winter's first real snow.

Our summer's guests still here: the roses and the geese

Hence, wanted I, your faith to raise me with release

But your kin and mine have left, and taken all their love

And death's e'er final sting would not relent, nor cease.

I prayed a prayer repentant, unto the God above

In hopes to be forgiven – with His undying love

For sins now past – I've rued the day – but sorrow still to keep,

And envy felt for tears now shed at that, your marker's feet.

Whose grave this is, I think I know: a man for whom, no none shall weep

Who now has plenty time to think – and eternity still to sleep.

Whose life that was, I think I know: a soul whose past none shall repeat

Who now has plenty time to think – and eternity still to sleep.

Autumn's Dance

The leaves of gold

And crimson red

That hug the earth

Now fallen dead

The wind that says,

"Winter is nigh"

Inviting to breathe

Till snow whispers, "Bye"

The cool crisp feel

Of the ground at your back

Covered in leaves

Once raked in a stack

Rapture of colors

Bring mist to the eye

Searching for words

But only a sigh

Days are now shorter

But filled with such joy

Each moment is cherished

Especially by boy

A season for strength

Dog days are gone

The cool air renews

And carries you on

On to enjoy

The wonders of life

Freeing the soul

From worry and strife

For now is the time

Partake in, last chance

The child-like pleasures

Of Autumn's sweet dance.

The Woodchopper

The man stands staring at the pile of wood – of maple, oak and pine,

He knows his family, tucked warm inside, won't pay his order any mind

He starts with the hardest, since he is still fresh – and leaves the pine till last,

Yet halfway through the knotty oak, he prays the pine and chore were past

His arms are aching, his back is stiff – it seems as though the wood has won,

He wonders how the pile has grown, and why the axe feels like a ton

Still, he lingers, a show to give, albeit as a mime – though all his anger, vented now

And then remembers, it's milking time! – thanks to his neighbor's friendly cow.

David. L. Mahan 46

Wedding Day

The hour was three in the afternoon, I will never forget. We had just come from our wedding reception, remember? Family and friends all assembled to wish us the best. Now they were all gone. It was just the two of us in your apartment. Our new home together. On the antique dresser, I noticed the array of photos in various sized frames – for the first time. The one that caught my attention was you, sitting by yourself at the beach. I wondered who had taken it. You had a look on your face of deep sadness – like a fountain of sorrow preserved forever in time. I started to ask you about the picture but stopped myself. I didn't need to know. I was glad your face was smiling now – at me. That was all that mattered. You studied me as I made my way to the chair across from you. As I sat down, you could sense I was troubled about something. "What is wrong?" you asked with compassion in your voice.

"My brother was certainly one tormented soul on his way out of this world," I replied, thinking of my visit with my brother, the day before, as he died. "He was filled with such anger and bitterness. It made me think of all we have to be thankful for."

"Do you mean, thank God?"

"Yes," I said, fidgeting in the chair somewhat. "I believe He's always looking out for us."

"I believe that also," you said, holding the crucifix necklace in your hand. "I know He loves us very much." You smiled as if to acknowledge we were one now.

"Are you comfortable?" you asked, standing up and walking toward me. As you came within inches of me, you knelt down, touching my legs in a familiar way. I reached my hand slowly toward your face and caressed it gently. There was a tenderness present. As I moved my hand down along your delicate cheekbone, caressing your regal neck, you moved closer, positioning your lips up to mine. We kissed. It was a kiss we had never experienced before. Perhaps it was *truly our first kiss*, I thought. It soon transformed into a long, deeply passionate kiss. The kind that was hard to distinguish where your face ended, and mine began. I realized then, we hadn't even kissed at the reception – except for the cutting of the cake. Oh, the joy of it and mess! The busyness of the formalities: the dance, the speeches, the tending to our guests.

Now as we kissed, I noticed your eyes were open, staring into mine. As if you were the reflection of my own fear and loneliness. Now, finally, preparing to vanish forever. As I stood up from the chair, I lifted you also, gently. You went willingly. Then picking you up fully in my arms, as a groom carries his bride across the threshold, I carried you toward the bed. We made love. We shared love in a way that was new and vulnerable for me. There was a genuine intimacy – free. Our bodies coalesced as one, in a sort of harmonious symphony. One that needed no choreographing. It was as though I was sharing my humanity, my imperfection, and you – the divine. When morning came, the sun was barely introducing itself through the open window. The gentle breeze from outside was swaying the curtains, like hands brushing away the past. We laid there together, both already awake, holding each other still in an embrace that said everything from *the fear was gone now – to hope for a future together was suddenly realized.*

David. L. Mahan 47

Grandchildren

Just yesterday, I came to know the truth of life and splendor told:

My six grand offspring to behold...

Elias, the gentle prophet; Theophan, the bold; Basil, the quiet, with greatness foretold;

Genevieve, the warrior; Elizabeth, the faithful; Gabriel, the confessor, God's praises extolled.

Each one – divine blessing from above, with God's imprint made

Reflecting His beauty and protection – hence, we all prayed.

Their joy is infectious, their wonder and love, a delight

Reminding us all – parents, grandparents, uncles, and aunts – to unite.

Their future – unique, brilliant and bright

Their hope is instilled in each of our lights.

We mustn't relinquish our God-given right

To speak into their hearts – truth and insight.

The Giant

I saw a giant arise today – of that to be quite sure

His rigid frame, ubiquitous eyes, and daunting stance,

His towering height did shadow endure,

Enticing the passersby to lingering glance.

At his feet, the traffic cop directed the flow

For such sight and commotion did bring

His presence was grand yet woeful to know,

Bestowing e'er progress – yet death's awful sting.

For death of the park, death of the meadows

Death of the flowering bed,

Death to the peaceful, calming repose –

Hence, the start of the neighborhood fled.

For how long and how much, of these towerin' giants allow,

Till life as we knew it – the past we once loved – is all but a memory now?

Insatiable

I witnessed the one side's passion today – the unprovoked attack.

The aggression; the Aggressor; the hatred; the disdain.

The fiery rockets in the air – descending – landing everywhere

Then came the screams; the destruction; and the devastating pain.

Then I watched as the pain from the other side awoke their passion: Revenge

Retaliation was swift and true – justice for them, yet with mercy to extend

It could've stopped there. But it didn't – the plight.

The vicious cycle continued – with no end in sight – no reason to comprehend.

We have seen this same fight – within our own soul – between wrong and right

And yet, we forge ahead – the wake of loss – relationships dead.

What is to become of the human soul when countless blessings do unfold,

Yet in the midst of realized dreams, songs of praise are squelched by screams?

Screams of hatred, screams of disdain – Masking the beauty, revealing such pain

Could it be the secret to joy and delight, is found in past wrongs now made right?

And contentment in forgiveness. Contentment not to fight.

For when you lose something (the honor) you cannot replace

When hope for the future is nowhere to trace

That is the time we must shed all hatred and fear,

And embrace God's love for humanity near.

David. L. Mahan 50

An Island Visited by Many Ships

Are you an island or firm mainland?

     Are you open for all to see?

And when the ships pass by, so grand,

     Do they feel greeted and welcomed be?

I am an island, that be my own will

     I shan't pretend to care too much

Whether ships pass by, or seas remain still,

     Yet I am the lonely – forsaking their touch

With offered pity, you showed me my err

     Venturing out: the dockhand, the sailor, the longshoreman to reach

They each have stories – hopes and dreams, and failures to share

     Each ship at bay – each life aboard – ne'er missed, ne'er breach.

From whence come to see, intertwined are we – the endless ships of the faithful

     Through trials and time, or family, or weakened souls of humanity

Made strong through pain, now shared, and promises kept willful,

     Divine appointments – each one unique – ever longing for community.

David. L. Mahan 51

The Good Fight

Come now, let us stand together – and face life's real enemy:

> The assailant's – fear and pride – insatiable need to win.

Let's stand as one, made strong by faith and will, with inherent brav'ry,

For we are not so different – you and me. We sail the same raging sea,

> On vessels made of truth and honor – of values e'er akin.

Yet lies foretold, and hatred bold, hath born in some a wall:

> Foul prejudice and spiteful ways, thus now we must destroy.

Hence, come, my friends, while time is here, and hope and faith are all

We need to still the tempest sea – division's fate, to fall

> And with compassion, understand, a brave new world employ.

David. L. Mahan 52

My Disappointment, When She Visits Me

That unwelcomed guest came calling today,
I bid her leave, though insist she did stay

Her presence did bring such a foul rancid smell,
I knew in an instant – of cure, none foretell

Reason did I, yes
A bargain to reach:
Expect no more, hence,
Then treaty not breach

Confront them not their failures,
For they had not forgotten them;
Instead, reflect on good things,
And on the hidden gems

For you are not I, and
We are not they
'Tis a trap for the lonely
To presume same will say

My trespasser, now gone
I sing soundly at peace,
If assign not a wrong –
Thereto, no caprice.

David. L. Mahan 53

Biography of Lucifer

His home, heaven's rapture

His favor none compare,

His melody, to capture

Angelic hosts declare

His stature, grand in splendor

Anointed cherub be,

Yet pride did thus destroy

Beholding his own beauty

Then rallied his legion

This once morning star,

Yet defeated was he

Vanquished ever far

How great the cost

Cast from heaven's glory

Paradise now lost

Hence, demonic rhapsody

Accuser, he became

Giving birth to all lies,

Condemned is he, the same

To hear eternal cries

David. L. Mahan 54

Hence, schemes, he plots
To thwart God's plan,
With fears and doubts
Yet safe in God's hand

The face of an angel –
The heart of a demon,
His wretched lot to tell –
His hell to remain in.

Misdirected Rage

I screamed at God today, with fist clinched and raised toward heaven; yet He simply replied,

"Come now, let us reason together." But I didn't want to – my anger now given.

I wanted to blame Him, someone, anyone but myself

For the regret now haunting me like a ghostly foul elf.

I stared at my face in the mirror. I didn't like what I'd see:

Eyes that refused to accept blame, err, or responsibility.

I felt that anger, once again, welling up, as when my parents died, many years hence

Except the difference then, there was no one to blame – life merely had no defense.

That was truly death's foul cheat

I couldn't blame them for falling asleep.

But now, I know I am the one – the only one – to accept the whole

For desperation felt and unbridled rage, now consuming my calloused soul.

My free will has brought me to this crossroad of Anguish or known Peace;

Hence, my free will can empower me to make the right choice – the choice of sweet release.

I must pick myself up, stand up straight. Brush off the dust of self-pity, and discard these old

Rags of shame, pride and regret.

I must put on the new self – with the clothing of humility, honesty, and mistakes now forget

I must own my destiny – no one else can.

This is a new day – it must be! A life-giving plan.

Essay on Grief

Loss is never easy to endure nor welcomed. However, there are certainly times when loss occurs and with it comes a prompt sense of understanding and even acceptance. An example would be an elderly member of the family passing away in their sleep, who has lived perhaps ninety years or more, and had a wonderfully fruitful life. In such an instance, while there is still sadness and grief experienced, the loss can be accepted relatively soon, and the life of the loved one celebrated with joy. The following focuses more on the issues that arise from grief that is more of a complicated or protracted nature.

One such example is when a child dies, whether due to an accident or disease, or for any reason. An inconceivable loss like that seems impossible to accept. Another type of complicated loss may be precipitated by a messy divorce. At times like these, it takes much longer to understand the reasons, if at all; hence, acceptance can be a long-drawn-out process. How one deals with this kind of painfully protracted and confusing grief is predicated upon various factors – such as regret. Carrying regret around, like a prisoner's ball and chain, only serves to take up valuable space in our soul where joy, peace, and contentment are waiting to abide.

Just as ghosts (if one believes in such) tend to linger due to unfinished business, grief often can linger beyond what is commonly expected. Albeit different for each person, the duration of the grieving process can be extended if there are unresolved issues that were not attended to prior to death. One of those factors might be the status of the relationship one had with the deceased prior to the loss. Another circumstance could be how much time there was, if any, to prepare and say good-bye. Regardless, complicated loss will usually be accompanied with regret and what-ifs. Regret is certainly a ghost that haunts from within and is quite often difficult to evict. The "exorcism" process can entail several various courses of action.

One such step might involve writing a letter to the deceased, I realize that sounds strange. But it helps sometimes to articulate what you should have said, or meant to say, when the loved one was still alive. Writing such sentiments is a wonderful way to reflect later on the growth and resolution that has transpired over time. Be honest with how you truly feel. Write what you would say if they were sitting in the room with you. Don't be concerned with syntax or structure – just express your heart toward them. Do it with the confidence that words have the power to affect change and heal – which they do.

Now, as we pass through the various stages of grief, the important thing to remember is everyone processes and experiences grief uniquely. While one may linger in the denial stage for an extended period of time, yet hardly even realize there is a stage called bargaining – another may accept the loss immediately, bypassing denial, yet spend what seems like an eternity dealing with the desolate fog of depression. Grief is an impetus, in and of itself. It cannot be reasoned or negotiated with. We stand no chance of placating its symptoms, nor appeasing its origin. Whatever control we may perceive having, in the end, our capitulation to the journey, however it looks, is all that is within our power.

David. L. Mahan 57

Grief is certainly not linear nor perspicuous. It is messy, erratic, and confusing at times. Its capricious nature is a task master that can leave one emotionally drained and discouraged. However, it is to our advantage, as the sojourner through the valley of grief, not to try and change our own experience of the journey – nor have expectations of how it should look and feel. But rather embrace and lean into the process, understanding as we do, the duration of the journey will most likely be shorter lived and perhaps even more meaningful in the end. As an old saying goes, "resistance is futile." The various stages of grief: denial, anger, bargaining, depression, and acceptance all have one thing in common, they are entirely unpredictable.

Darkness Pending –

The impending death of either a loved one or oneself is an extremely arduous and painful experience to process and navigate through. Certainly, deserving of the utmost compassion. Uniquely different from a death of a loved one who has already passed, anticipated death is rife with ambivalent emotions. Watching someone we deeply care for, and love, suffer through the anguish of a fatal illness, is an experience never to be forgotten. The key here is to try to focus on the opportunity to communicate and express feelings of love, appreciation and affirmation to the appropriate person, rather than focus on the impending loss. I realize this is much easier said than done. However, expressing these feelings while still possible is an opportunity that if missed could lead to regret for many years to come. The famous cliché "seize the day" could never be more relevant than here, nor more urgent than now.

Here, I believe, the ministry of presence is of the utmost value. Too often, we feel uncomfortable, not knowing what is best to say, so we end up avoiding the person who desperately wants and needs our comforting presence. I learned early on when my parents died, after the funeral and burial was over, and all the subsequent business affairs were resolved, the family and friends who lingered still, and were simply present just to sit with me, were what helped me navigate my grief more than anything else. Therefore, if the grief is impending, yet not fully imposed, the willingness to devote your time and your presence could be the very tonic of peace and comfort they desperately need.

Wounded Grief –

The grief process can become thwarted and, in turn, slow down the transition period – resulting in delayed healing and acceptance. Certainly, if there were unresolved issues with the departed, such as unforgiveness, harsh words spoken, betrayal, or abandonment, then unless those things are rectified and resolved somehow the wound of grief may never fully heal. I am not speaking of a healing that involves forgetfulness – neither of the offense nor the loss. What I am referring to is a healing of acceptance – of wholeness. It is a healing that results in a true inner peace that passes all understanding. Although the person may be gone from this world, you are still here. And you must find a way to reach closure, accept the loss, and attain lasting peace. The most effective way to achieve this is by leaning into the process, not running away.

Hope Renewed

That winter's eve, I came to find
      The gladheart'd man I'd left behind
'Midst snow-drenched pine, and oak leaves ling'ring
      I heard the sound of church bells ringing.

At once, I knew I'd found at last
      The hope – to marry – with cherished past
A hope for future, firm with grace
      A past where shame could be erased.

Though passion – through fear – had slipped away
      Rekindled love for nature dear,
Thus, bid me now to ever stay
      And harkened true zeal to now adhere.

For where I'd strayed away from path
      My soul had journeyed through place of wrath
Yet, fear now dead, and I am free
      To deeply live – serenity.

Now Springs of hope and life renewed
      Beckoning me to peace construed.
Hence, I shall live where I once felt –
      Alive, reborn – this poet dwelt.

David. L. Mahan 59

A Beautiful Riot

As we strolled 'long the lake shore, with sullen sky in shades of grey

I thought to wait, for skies to clear – perhaps some other day

      But you marveled at shades of brilliant red, of brazen yellow and of gold

The riot of colors took us back to when on earth we used to say,

      "Our hope was in love, life together – and faith ever bold."

Just then we saw the horse-drawn carriage, by the marsh, standing still

The anticipation we both felt – was governing our will

      We climbed aboard, with playful hearts, eagerly like children

In search of fond memories – the distant and thrill

      Spontaneity our guide now, reminding us of when.

"When?" The saintly driver asked us, "And where to go?"

Knowing how days turned into years, with nothing to show

      We both replied at once, "Anywhere in the past."

We pondered then, why, we'd ever come to know,

      A longing to espouse such feelings downcast?

Perhaps it was failure, or perhaps pure neglect

That brought us to the choice – that glad fall epoch

      A choice to embrace our paradise found, no longer dismay

Or maybe we slumbered, complacently suspect

      Whatever the case, we knew love would win, foretelling the way.

You remarked how my hair was now greyer than brown

Touching the back, the length and thinning crown,

　　I said life had cursed all the dark, leaving only the grey

More distinguished was I, you said with no frown

　　Your smile dispelling doubtful cares away.

I asked what you'll miss the most – though paradise be just fine

You told me how you loved those books – the riot of learning – all different kind

　　The yearning for poems filled with sweet verse, that's what I'll miss

The bookshop and library, the reading chair – more time

　　I wished I had read more, though writing was bliss!

We jumped off the carriage, making harness bells shake

The riot of joy in us, that day by the lake

　　Rekindling the truth we'd held so dear: "We're the kids," you exclaimed!

In a duvet of scarlet, we rolled down the hill, erasing our mistakes –

　　Dismissing the echo of past sins – unnamed.

We held each other close 'neath the blanket and quilt

Then wished away shame, fear and sorrow, un-wilt

　　And pledged our resolve once again: to be lover, soulmate and faithful friend.

Nothing was asked. Yet everything given – our future now built

　　The riot of grace besieging us that heavenly day . . . would hence never end.

Paradise Found

How long have I been sleeping, drifting along this endless train of metal coffins?
Hoping I could earn your gratitude and grace.

I am awakened by your steadfast relent – no rejection, ne'er to trace.

The words I have lived to offer, with pen and with sweet verse, cannot begin to mean as much –
As my lover's faithful touch.

For a martyr is never fully satisfied. No sin can be erased.

I looked at myself today – seeing the man I once was, looking back – not knowing whom I had become.

Do you still recognize me? I fear my God doesn't anymore; hence, to fear I now succumb.

Yet deep within the crevasses of my hardened soul, there is light still, fighting its way out.
The provoked tears – the capricious lament.

Can you see it? I desperately want to!

Then as those words of truth find their way onto this paper, I know there must be hope –

For I am still breathing. I can still shout.

God hasn't given up on me yet. To this task, He remains unbent.

Teach me unconditioned love. Help me as I bear myself, fully at your feet.

Arm me with the tools I need: the skills I have to wield.

Teach me to surrender – to lose – but never then to yield. Help me not retreat.

Open my eyes to the wonder of each day. Rend my heart with honest Joy, I pray.

I yearn to see the beauty in the simple, the failure – in serenity's decoy.
The beauty in the chaos. And hidden Paradise, lost.

Help me use the past, these scars as steppingstones to employ – to Paradise found at any cost.

Essay on Purpose

Perhaps the wisest thing we can do once we sense a "calling" to a specific purpose, is to engage a team of trusted friends and family to seek the LORD together for discernment and confirmation. Or, if the reader does not adhere to the belief in a divine Deity, then perhaps recruiting the same group of friends and family for advice and counsel is better said. Too often, we rush to the assumption we have heard the voice of God (or whatever serves as our "plumb line"), only to discover what we heard was our own personal desires or goals. I realize sometimes we get it right on our own and hear direction calling accurately. However, there is nothing lost in asking others closest to us to come along side and seek out discernment and peace as well. A helpful hint in this pivotal quest: search your heart for your true passion.

I believe the reason for reluctance here is usually fear – what if they hear something different? This is where it is crucial to seek the right people to aid in the process – people who have demonstrated over time they truly have a maturity and wisdom that comes from years of living well and have proven they provide sound counsel. We should never choose someone who will merely cater to our own predilections or selfish agendas. It is crucial to remain open to possibly being wrong. In other words, don't let pride or an individual penchant cloud your ability to receive what the other person is hearing. They might just be right.

Testing the waters, as the old saying suggests, is a highly recommended next step. There is no greater surety than trying something on for size – whether new clothing or a new direction in life. Typically, the answer will be expeditiously provided by way of a "good fit" or not. If the result of the well-meaning test is the latter, then we should not lose heart, but rather pick ourselves up and try something different. As the famous president, Theodore Roosevelt, was known for saying:

"….The credit belongs to the man who is actually in the arena, whose face is marred by dust and sweat and blood; who strives valiantly; who errs, who comes short again and again, because there is no effort without error and shortcoming; but who does actually strive to do the deeds; who knows great enthusiasms, the great devotions; who spends himself in a worthy cause; who at the best knows in the end the triumph of high achievement, and who at the worst, if he fails, at least fails while daring greatly, so that his place shall never be with those cold and timid souls who neither know victory nor defeat." Remember, regret is a ghost that haunts from within.

Patience is of the utmost necessity when going through the discernment stage. It is inherent for each of us to want to know the answer as fast as possible. Waiting can be an extremely challenging proposition. However, just like taking our time to do a job the right way the first time is prudent, thereby avoiding having to do it twice, so also taking the extra time at the beginning to ensure we are truly acting with prudence will pay dividends in the end. The time we spend in the 'in-between-place' of consequence due to haste will always be a longer duration than simply waiting in advance for God-given discernment and faith. Our God-given purpose is well worth the wait!

David. L. Mahan 63

Eulogy of A Tree

I walk beneath the towerin' trees,

Who offer up forgiving breeze.

Though it is I whom they resent;

Their death and destruction I have lent.

The seed, the sapling, now e'er forgot

Through thoughtless caring, the hollow rot;

If only time could be turned back,

When all was borrowed: mere wood stack.

The home thus built with stacking stone,

And mortar, clay and sand alone.

A roof with thatch of straw and hay,

To save the wheat for threshing day.

Instead, with reckless axe and saw

And no regard for planting seed,

Before the frost, after the thaw,

The culprit leaving only reed.

Hence with no mind, rapacious act

We thus, in turn, abandon pact:

Made with our God to steward be,

Yet forfeit future carelessly.

David. L. Mahan 64

For how long shall we tarry,

Imprisoned on this mortal earth?

If hands full of greed we carry

And precious beauty no more to birth,

Hence e'er neglecting God's gifted worth:

The mighty oak; the gentle pine;

The sprawling spruce - the Christmas kind;

The brilliant maple; the shivering aspen;

The weeping willow; and cherry bastion.

Though modern ways and means impart

Though bridges span and railways start

And mankind's neighbor so close about,

No need there be to ever shout.

Still wretched be our woeful lot – If in the end, trees . . . we're without.

David. L. Mahan 65

Words Unspoken

Madness, some might call it;

I prefer the word, sadness – or beguiled.

Either way, I reckon it started that night those unwelcomed words came calling . . .

About his loved ones, their unexpected dying.

I recollect him, lying there on the floor, undone, crying –

Groping for the words to say.

Anything to heal, away.

But nothing came unfurled;

Just the feeling he was slipping deep into a darker world,

Where words became like ghosts: ever haunting.

Maybe *it was* a kind of madness, ever daunting –

Some folks would call it that.

One sister thought as much, insofar as what was spoken;

Those were her words, more or less, unbroken.

The other kin, a breath of fresh air and caress –

To his heartsick: a healing balm and tonic.

Yet now, nigh twoscore winters the latter, don't much more now even matter

What words weren't said, or should've been;

Only what isn't said now, that's what's seen.

She'd rather it never happen – the knowing, that is.

Too uncomfortable, those were her words.

I'd've rather she'd said, "Too bad."

Or simply, "Sorry."

I can still see the young man lying there on the floor crying himself to sleep,

Wondering how or whom he'd wake up and beseech.

Then the older man emerged, the next morn:

A stranger, troubled, now forlorn –

Wanting to be heard.

Can you hear him?

One moment, heartfelt praises of ovation; the next, curse full chides of condemnation.

His words – like fiery darts or healing parts – are only heard now

Through his verse or melancholy prose, save his own tortured soul who knows.

His lament tells him now what to say – or his God – in utter bleak dismay.

Nonetheless, they are words of profound significance,

Or perhaps to him, are merely his own impetus.

Maybe it truly is pure madness,

When regrets do unhinge one's gladness.

When you confronted death, did you do it word-empty-handed?

I know that he did. Hence, upon his heart, healing never landed.

And I hate when the words are 'ever left unsaid;

And I hated, and hate the silence of the dead.

Postulation

Ah, dear Mr. Frost, I realize, "It was treason," you once said, "to bow and accept the end of a

love or a season;"

But what may I ask, is a soul to do when the love or a season has become

The very prison or painful chain to some – keeping one from experiencing true joy;

Or preventing them from discovering the secret answer to employ

That cultivates the very freedom and peace that defies all reason?

May I offer instead a suggestion I once read: that waiting too long,

Can deprive a soul of its true inner song; hence, leave them never knowing the way

To set sail, with reckless abandon, and capture their destiny by heaving astay: the anchor of their

perplexing dismay.

So, isn't the far greater treason to bow and accept the welcome of one's own demons?

For though it is fear which hath in many a hearts been born,

'Tis acceptance of fate that maketh the human soul forlorn.

David. L. Mahan 68

Alone, My Song Sings Loudly

Alone, my song sings loudly; its message fills my soul –

    Engendered by a longing: A hope to know my God.

Whilst tempest's shouts and demons rage, my peace can still unfold;

Hence, life's stalwart stands ever strong, though torrent waves do roll.

    Thus, I shall venture life's trodden path ne'er veering wide nor broad.

You came to me with reasoning for which I was to stay

    With family and with friendship; however, mute may be.

Yet it is in my solitude, my voice can sing away;

And only in my hidden place are demons held at bay.

    So, I shall linger – I shall 'bide – where I may live freely.

And if my heartfelt pining may cause you foul umbrage,

    Or whence my reasons' timing doth bring no recompense –

I shan't be forlorn, nay penitent for wanting my own cage

Of peaceful homage nature paid; hence, poet thus a sage.

    For I shall welcome Worship's song: Alive in God's presence.

David. L. Mahan 69

Free Will

Free will – you can have it!
The irascible man said, beset.
He said it while looking out over the devastating destruction the war had just cost – both sides:
The irreversible death, the pain and the despair.

For those who want to believe a sovereign God bestows this gift of free will solely for our
benefit . . .
I am reluctantly happy for you.
Although, after six decades of living, I have witnessed all too many examples of its fallout;

A price too costly: rapacious dealings; self-indulgent motives; and vengeful retribution.
All these results of free will are merely the by-product of that age-old enemy:
The human condition.

How can it be the same hand that holds the newborn babe, or caresses the lover's face,
Also is the hand that strikes that same face or pushes the button that kills innocent lives?

Robots? – You ask then? No, that is not my wish.
For to set sail on the open sea; to climb the highest peak; or compose an opus that inspires
Out of one's own inclination and determination is a wonderful thing.

But then, where is the compromise – where is the balance?
Where is the middle ground?
Do we accept the fallacious notion that to enjoy such divine blessings
We must accept the evil curses as well?

Never!
We must seek to find higher ground – to strive, to love and not to yield.
Perhaps the answer is in a Higher Power.
Perhaps the answer is found in the question: What or Whom do we worship?

David. L. Mahan 70

Colorado Christmas

Colorado splendor with wondrous delight, captures my senses and saturates my sight...

Pristine Pine and fragile Aspen beckon me to write

Red Oak and Blue Spruce boasting of their strength

Open fields of snow with haystacks in furlong length

Guernsey cows grazing, invoking deep breath

Capricious blizzards and latent frost threatening now fall's death

Bigtooth Sugar Maple awesome to behold

Paper Birch and Purple Ash, colors enchanted bold

Roaring rivers and generous creeks evoking repose

Rocky mountain rambles, daring in late snows

Crackling fireplace and hot toddies

Sleigh rides with warm bodies

Swooshing down fresh ski slopes, exhilarating thrill

Scent of fresh cut Balsam Fir doth peace e'er instill

Snowmen and Ice forts inspiring chilled quakes

Grey geese and mallards invading crystal lakes

Magpies and Bluejays christening snow laden branches

Graceful Gulls o'erhead making elegant advances

Winter's requiem doth engender faith, hence quelching all debate

Of all the magic wonders found within the Centennial State.

David. L. Mahan 71

Essay on Affirmation and Attitude

Planting seeds of praise and thanksgiving will always usher us into a place of focusing on the things of God and of His creation in this world. This posture provides us with greater insight and discernment into what the proper, positive response should be to whatever the conundrum is we're wrestling with at the time. Praise and worship clear our mind and heart of things that are clouding our judgment and preventing us from hearing the voice of reason and clarity.

These things may, in fact, be normal, innocuous things—such as how to balance our budget, how to motivate our kids to try harder in school, or maybe how to tell our spouse we don't appreciate the way they're treating us. Yet again, they may be persistent temptations or recurring fears we can't seem to overcome. Either way, whatever the source of the distraction or confusion, nothing will provide greater clarity and perception than entering into God's glorious nature, and enjoying creation, with a humble and open spirit. Once we're in that secret place of worship and communion both with Creator and His creation, we can find true rest and peace for our weary souls. Working in one's garden, taking an extended hike through nature's classroom, or simply resting on the porch in the cool of the day, watching life's parade are all excellent ways to remind oneself of why we're here and, in turn, evoke the right attitude of gratitude.

Praise and worship are the one sure way to humble ourselves and recognize that God is the center of the universe—and not us. Even "praising" and honoring others for their noble attributes and accomplishments is a great way to remind oneself of our own imperfection and humanity. I would liken the ones we love, such as our spouse or children, to a beautiful garden. If we don't tend to that garden with a loving and sedulously careful approach, then that garden could become sick (heartsick) and lose its beauty and joy-evoking presence. The best way to cultivate and maintain the beautiful "gardens" in the lives that God has entrusted us with is by paying tribute to and honoring them with both endearing words and acts of love and recognition.

Affirming our loved ones daily will build up their sense of worth and value like nothing else can. After all, we are called to be our Creator's hands and mouth, speaking His words of life and love. We must always be cognizant of what's dying around us. To discern what's being choked out by thorns of bitterness or neglect; what is in dire need of water and nourishment; and what is lacking in the sunshine of our own presence and attention. Speak words of praise, gratitude, and affirmation, first and foremost to our God; and then, in turn, with that divine flow of love exuding from our hearts, speak words of affirmation, gratitude, and affection to the ones whom God places in our life's journey.

Since there are no guarantees concerning tomorrow, shouldn't we focus our attention and energy on today and its bountiful blessings? Learn from the past, hope for the future, but live in the moment. Today is the gift from God that needs to be opened with a joyful and grateful heart.

David. L. Mahan 72

A Tribute to Dave

Recently, a very dear friend of mine passed away after a hard-fought battle with cancer. His name was Dave. Seldom in life is one ever fortunate enough to meet a truly noble person – my friend, Dave was such a person. A man whose character exemplified integrity and humility like no one else I have ever known. His strong faith, infectious optimism and ability to breathe inspiration into a person's soul, motivating them to aspire to be better than before, all the while still making them feel accepted, was truly a God-given gift.

Even in the midst of a highly stressful and challenging industry, known as construction, Dave had an innate sense of what mattered most – the human element. He clearly loved helping others rise above the frustrating and even capricious aspects of everyday life to become stronger and more compassionate – a combination that is not commonplace in our society today. Yet for Dave, his inner strength came from his inherent ability to appreciate people for who they were, and where they were in life, but care for them too much to leave them there.

Dave blessed my life in more ways than I will ever be able to sufficiently communicate. Knowing him as a trusted friend and mentor sharpened my character and helped mold me to be a better man – father, husband, brother, and worker. I will forever be in his debt for the way he poured himself into my journey of life. He truly personified the famous quote of Abraham Lincoln, "When we look for the good in others, expecting to find it, we most certainly will." That is Dave's legacy to me – and to so many others, who are better for having known him.

Another quote that epitomized Dave's life message was from General George Patton, "Never fail to honor your people. When a true leader's work is complete and his aim is fulfilled, his people should say and believe, we did this ourselves." Dave understood the concept of honoring and affirming others. His self-effacing leadership style, leading by example and inspiration, will always be remembered, and emulated by many.

The Bible verse in Romans 12:10, "Honor one another above yourselves," was truly portrayed in how Dave interacted with everyone he came in contact with. He had a way of making a person feel they were valued, appreciated, and important merely by greeting them. His intentional way of making time for others – whether it was an encouraging word of advice, a listening ear, or an affirming compliment – I marveled at how many times I was blessed to be the recipient of his life-energizing presence.

During the thirty years I was honored to be called his friend, I watched Dave carry himself with the upmost grace and poise through some very challenging times at work and in personal life. Schedule changes, contractual issues, or other unforeseen difficulties in our business, as well as the illness he faced courageously head on, all of which could bring most men to a breaking point, only seemed to make Dave's light shine brighter. He had a truly amazing knack for seeing an obstacle or adversity as an opportunity to be even more optimistic. This was magnified by his intelligent and creative approach to finding solutions – when others only saw defeat. His ameliorating humor during difficult times was always a welcomed reminder to keep things in proper perspective.

One of the many ways he impacted my life was shortly after we became friends and started working together. I was struggling through my own 'in between place' after my parents' death, just a few years before, and divorce from my first marriage, which had just ended. Dave was there when I needed a friend to listen, to simply care and show support, to offer advice when appropriate, but mostly just to be there. He truly helped me pull some deeply rooted 'weeds' out of my life that were holding me back, which, in turn, accelerated my journey through transition into a place of abiding peace.

I will forever be a better person – more hopeful, affirming, and caring – simply because of knowing Dave and being his friend. My heartfelt prayer is that one day I will impact someone with the same probity and positive perspective on life. I thank God for Dave's life – his example and unyielding purpose – and for the impact he had on mine.

David. L. Mahan 74

Thoreau's Vision

I met a man today, whose bellicose manner seemed quite astray.

His desperation, silent though, beneath his anger did convey.

I queried him for reason why, tempestuous ways did imply

A lack of peace and solicitude – a love for life did he deny.

"Why are you full of such dismay?"

      "My hope is gone, so far away."

"Is there no purpose left in thee?"

      "I have no vision, nor destiny."

Just then, I thought on what the Good Book said,

      "When vision is gone, men perish."

At once, I realized his heart was dark – devoid of love to cherish.

He had spent his life on futile search; hence, answering wrong call:

To please all others. Then 'membering Thoreau – his admonishment to all:

If one's own music be unique, if drummer be of different kind,

Thus, let us each keep step with what we hear; hence, peace, in turn, to find.

I walked away, forlorn, distraught, consumed with such pity

For the man in this sad story, was really only me.

David. L. Mahan 75